AFTER AN ADVENTURE IN DEEP SPACE, THE
ORIGINAL X-MEN RETURNED TO EARTH,
CHANGED BY THEIR EXPERIENCES...

X-MEN BLUE

SURVIVING THE EXPERIENCE

Writer/**CULLEN BUNN**
Artists/**NATHAN STOCKMAN** (#29-30),
JORGE MOLINA (#31),
ANDRÉS GENOLET (#32)
& **MARCUS TO** (#33-36)
Color Artist/**MATT MILLA**
Letterer/**VC's JOE CARAMAGNA**
Cover Art/**R.B. SILVA** with
RAIN BEREDO (#29-34)
& **MATT MILLA** (#35-36)

Assistant Editor/**CHRIS ROBINSON**
Editor/**DARREN SHAN**
X-Men Group Editors/**MARK PANICCIA** & **JORDAN D. WHITE**

X-MEN CREATED BY **STAN LEE** & **JACK KIRBY**

Collection Editor/**JENNIFER GRÜNWALD** • Assistant Editor/**CAITLIN O'CONNELL**
Associate Managing Editor/**KATERI WOODY** • Editor, Special Projects/**MARK D. BEAZLEY**
VP Production & Special Projects/**JEFF YOUNGQUIST** • SVP Print, Sales & Marketing/**DAVID GABRIEL**
Book Designer/**JAY BOWEN**

Editor in Chief/**C.B. CEBULSKI** • Chief Creative Officer/**JOE QUESADA**
President/**DAN BUCKLEY** • Executive Producer/**ALAN FINE**

X-MEN BLUE VOL. 5: SURVIVING THE EXPERIENCE. Contains material originally published in magazine form as X-MEN BLUE #29-36. First printing 2018. ISBN 978-1-302-90980-2. Published by MARVEL WORLDWIDE, INC., a subsidiary of MARVEL ENTERTAINMENT, LLC. OFFICE OF PUBLICATION: 135 West 50th Street, New York, NY 10020. Copyright © 2018 MARVEL No similarity between any of the names, characters, persons, and/or institutions in this magazine with those of any living or dead person or institution is intended, and any such similarity which may exist is purely coincidental. **Printed in the U.S.A.** DAN BUCKLEY, President, Marvel Entertainment; JOHN NEE, Publisher; JOE QUESADA, Chief Creative Officer; TOM BREVOORT, SVP of Publishing; DAVID BOGART, SVP of Business Affairs & Operations, Publishing & Partnership; DAVID GABRIEL, SVP of Sales & Marketing, Publishing; JEFF YOUNGQUIST, VP of Production & Special Projects; DAN CARR, Executive Director of Publishing Technology; ALEX MORALES, Director of Publishing Operations; DAN EDINGTON, Managing Editor; SUSAN CRESPI, Production Manager; STAN LEE, Chairman Emeritus. For information regarding advertising in Marvel Comics or on Marvel.com, please contact Vit DeBellis, Custom Solutions & Integrated Advertising Manager, at vdebellis@marvel.com. For Marvel subscription inquiries, please call 888-511-5480. **Manufactured between 9/7/2018 and 10/9/2018 by LSC COMMUNICATIONS, KENDALLVILLE, IN, USA.**

10 9 8 7 6 5 4 3 2 1

**CENTENNIAL PARK
BRANCH**

SOMETHING WRONG WITH YOUR BEER, HONEY?

HMM--?

YOU'VE BEEN NURSING IT ALL NIGHT.

IF YOU DON'T LIKE IT, I CAN POUR YOU SOMETHING ELSE.

SOMETHING WITH A LITTLE MORE *KICK,* MAYBE?

"--NOT FROM AROUND HERE."

DON'T
T IT TOUCH
YOU!

SLLLLLLSH!

AAAGGH!

SHRA-GHKT-KLK-TRK-KLCK!

P-PLEASE.
DON'T
HURT ME.

JUST...
JUST LEAVE
US ALONE.

JIMMY HUDSON IS TILL PART OF WHO YOU ARE.

YOU'RE NOT THE MAN YOU WERE, BUT THERE'S SOMETHING THAT MAKES YOU *DIFFERENT* FROM THE OTHER POISONS.

YOU'VE CHANGED.

IT'S BOTH PHYSIOLOGICAL AND MENTAL.

I SENSE IT.

SO DO YOU.

THESE ARE JUST THE PREVIOUS HOST'S MEMORIES.

THEY ARE NOT MINE.

JIMMY HUDSON IS *DEAD*.

I DON'T THINK SO.

STAY OUT OF MY MIND.

YOU WILL NOT LIKE WHAT YOU SEE.

TOLD YOU.

THOSE...ARE MEMORIES...

...OF OTHER WORLDS...

...OTHER REALITIES THE POISONS CONQUERED...

GOOD TIMES.

YOU GO DIGGING FOR THE *OLD* HOST'S THOUGHTS...

...YOU GET THE *NEW* HOST'S THOUGHTS, TOO!

CHUNK!

SH-CHUNK!

THK!

THRASH!

THRASH!

AAGGH!

SLLISH!

SGLK!

JEAN!

JEAN GREY WOULD *DESTROY* ME.

SHE WOULD KILL THE *LAST* OF MY KIND.

JUST AS SHE KILLED THE *FIRST*.

SHE *DESERVES* TO DIE.

I CAN'T WAIT ANY LONGER.

I'M ACTIVATING THESE REMOTE *ANTI-VENOM* MODULES.

THEY'LL KILL HIM ON CONTACT.

I'M SORRY, JIMMY.

SO SORRY.

BUT YOU GIVE ME NO CHOICE.

ARE YOU SURE, BEAST?

I'M BETTING I'M *FASTER* THAN YOU THINK.

DROP THEM.

TH-THUMP

LET HER GO, JIMMY.

CALL ME BY MY *TRUE* NAME.

ALL RIGHT...*POISON*... WHATEVER YOU WANT TO BE CALLED.

YOU CAN GO, ALL RIGHT?

I GIVE YOU MY WORD.

LET JEAN GO, AND WE'LL LEAVE YOU BE.

BUT JEAN GREY STILL HAS *HOPE* FOR THE PREVIOUS HOST.

AND SHE IS ONE OF THE ONLY PEOPLE TO RESIST OUR INFLUENCE.

I'D BE BETTER OFF KILLING--

I THINK...
I THINK SHE'LL BE ALL RIGHT.

I CAN'T HELP MYSELF.

IT'S LIKE I HAVE...I DUNNO...TWO SETS OF THOUGHTS... TWO SETS OF MEMORIES...IN MY HEAD.

AND THEY'RE TRYING TO KILL EACH OTHER.

DUDE.

WE WANT TO HELP.

BUT YOU KNOW I HAVE TO ICE YOU UP OR SOMETHING, RIGHT?

DON'T BOTHER, BOBBY.

SHGGGKT

30

DAKEN--? WHAT DO YOU THINK YOU'RE DOING?

CALL IT AN ASSASSINATION, CYCLOPS.

CALL IT A MERCY KILLING.

CALL IT SIBLING RIVALRY.

THE END RESULT'S THE SAME...

...JIMMY HUDSON DIES TODAY.

D-DON'T CALL ME THAT. THAT'S NOT MY NAME. NOT ANYMORE.

POISON. I'M THE LAST... POISON.

IN A FEW SECONDS, IT WON'T MATTER WHAT I CALL YOU, "BROTHER."

UNLESS, OF COURSE, SOMEONE SPRINGS FOR A TOMBSTONE.

STAY BACK! WE'RE NOT GOING TO LET YOU HURT HIM!

WOOOOOSSH!

YOU... STUBBORN DAMN KIDS.

NNN--

JIMMY HUDSON DIED WHEN THE POISONS TOOK HIM.

WHO... DO YOU THINK THAT IS?

HE'S AN X-MAN.

SHRAKKOW!

BLOODSTORM!

I AM SORRY ABOUT THIS, DAKEN.

JIMMY HUDSON STRUGGLES AGAINST A TERRIBLE DARKNESS.

THIS IS SOMETHING I UNDERSTAND.

SOMETHING I INTEND TO HELP HIM FACE.

I CAN CATCH HIM.

ANGEL-- WAIT. I DON'T THINK *ANY* OF US SHOULD GO AFTER JIMMY *ALONE.*

GOOD ADVICE. LEAVE MY BROTHER TO THOSE WHO CAN HANDLE HIM EFFECTIVELY.

YOU MEAN-- YOU'RE GONNA KILL HIM.

DON'T GO CHANGING, BOBBY. THAT ADORABLE, DIM-WITTED DOOFINESS WILL SERVE YOU WELL IN LIFE.

WHAT'S THIS ALL ABOUT?

DID MAGNETO *REALLY* SEND YOU AFTER JIMMY?

TELL US WHY HE'D DO SOMETHING LIKE THAT.

MAKE ME.

IF YOU INSIST.

JEAN... MAYBE WE SHOULD--

NEEAAAGH!

UH--

S-SORRY ABOUT THAT, GUYS.

HE HAD SOME SORT OF PSI-DEFENSE TRAINING.

HE TURNED MY OWN POWERS AGAINST ME.

GUYS-- DID YOU SEE WHERE HE WENT?

HAI!

FWUMP!

IS THAT...
...ALL...
...YOU'VE GOT?

OKAY. NICE THAT EVERYONE KNOWS WHERE THEY STAND.

JIMMY... *POISON*... LET'S YOU AND ME HAVE A WORD.

THAT *THING* IS NOT YOUR FRIEND, JEAN!

IT'S VICIOUS AND VIOLENT AND ALONE!

IT'S MORE *DANGEROUS* THAN YOU CAN IMAGINE!

QUIET, YOU. WE'LL TALK *LATER.*

YOU SHOULD *LISTEN* TO HIM.

HE'S RIGHT ABOUT ME.

YOU LOOK AT ME, AND YOU SEE YOUR *TEAMMATE*...BUT THAT'S ONLY BECAUSE IT'S WHAT YOU WANT TO SEE.

I DON'T BELIEVE THAT.

WHAT ARE YOU DOING?

IT'S ALL RIGHT, SCOTT. I'VE GOT THIS.

LET HIM GO.

WHAT?

ARE YOU SURE?

I MEAN... HE *DID* JUST TRY TO KILL YOU.

JEAN-- THIS ISN'T A GOOD IDEA.

IT'S *MY* CALL, SCOTT.

OUT OF ALL OF US, I *KNOW* WHAT HE'S GOING THROUGH.

HE'S JIMMY.

HE'S *STILL* JIMMY.

KRRN- KRK- KRMMBLE

JEAN... I...

YOU WANNA TAKE A WALK?

...SURE.

THERE'S ALL THESE THOUGHTS...THESE MEMORIES...RUNNING THROUGH MY HEAD.

UP UNTIL I WAS...*TAKEN*...I COULDN'T REMEMBER ANYTHING.

NOW, IT'S ALL COMING BACK, BUT IT'S LIKE...I DON'T KNOW...LIKE MY LIFE FLASHING BEFORE MY EYES.

ONLY IT'S MORE THAN ONE LIFE.

WHAT AM I, JEAN?

WHEN THE POISON HIVE TOOK ME...

...I FELT LIKE I WAS DROWNING...IN MY MEMORIES...IN THE WILL OF THE HIVE ITSELF.

AND I HAD TO FIGHT TO HOLD ONTO SOME LITTLE SHRED OF THE PERSON I WAS.

I STITCHED MYSELF BACK TOGETHER USING TELEKINESIS AND WHATEVER GENETIC MATTER WAS LEFT OVER INSIDE THE POISON ARMOR THAT SURROUNDED ME.

I'M NOT SURE WHAT YOU ARE, JIMMY...

...BUT I KNOW YOU'RE MY *FRIEND*.

AND I'M NOT GOING TO HOLD YOU PRISONER. I'M NOT GOING TO HUNT YOU DOWN.

YOU'RE A GOOD PERSON, AND IF YOU NEED SOME SPACE TO HELP YOU FIGURE THAT OUT...

...THEN TAKE ALL THE SPACE YOU NEED.

THAT WAS **STUPID.** YOU REALIZE THAT, RIGHT?

HE'S NOT JIMMY HUDSON ANYMORE. HE'S SOMETHING WORSE... SOMETHING THAT'S GOING TO HURT PEOPLE.

TELL ME ABOUT MAGNETO.

HEH. MAKE ME.

I'M NOT PLAYING THAT GAME AGAIN. I DON'T HAVE TO.

BOBBY--

DUDE...DON'T MAKE ME USE MY ICE TO CRUSH THE LIFE OUT OF YOU.

IT'LL RUIN MY REP AS A **LOVEABLE DOOF.**

MAYBE MAGNETO IS WRONG ABOUT YOU. MAYBE YOU DO HAVE WHAT IT TAKES WHEN IT COMES TIME TO PLAY HARDBALL.

MAYBE YOU LEARNED SOMETHING FROM HIM AFTER ALL.

AT LEAST... WHEN IT DOESN'T INVOLVE YOUR PET WOLVERINE.

WHAT'S MAGNETO PLAYING AT?

OH, HE'S **DONE** PLAYING.

HE JUST WANTED ME TO DEAL WITH JIMMY-BOY WHILE HE TACKLED **BIGGER** TARGETS.

YOU LEAVING HIM HIGH AND DRY...MOTHERVINE... THE POISONS...THE OLD GUY'S RUN ALL OUT OF PATIENCE.

HE'S TAKIN THE FIGHT STRAIGHT T ANYONE HE FE IS A DANGER MUTANTS.

FIRST ON THE CHOPPING BLOCK--

--THE **WHITE QUEEN** HERSELF.

31

HEY, ALEX.

LORNA. THANKS FOR COMING.

FEELS *STRANGE*, DOESN'T IT?

BEING YOURSELF AFTER SO MUCH TIME BEING... *SOMEONE ELSE*.

IT FEELS LIKE...I OWE EVERYONE AN *APOLOGY*.

YOU WEREN'T YOURSELF.

I WASN'T BEING CONTROLLED. I WASN'T BRAINWASHED.

THE WAY I WAS...PART OF THAT WAS *ME*.

PART OF ME *WANTED* TO DO THE THINGS I DID.

I THOUGHT IT WAS THE RIGHT THING TO DO.

I FIGURE MAGNETO'S COMING AFTER ME NOW.

MAYBE THAT'S WHAT I DESERVE.

I DON'T KNOW WHAT MY FATHER'S PLANNING, ALEX.

BUT--WHETHER YOU REALIZE IT OR NOT--I'M GUESSING HE KNOWS YOU WEREN'T IN TOTAL CONTROL OF YOUR SENSES.

YOU SHOULD SIT THIS ONE OUT, X-MEN.

LET ERIK DO HIS THING.

SOON ENOUGH, IT WILL BE OUT OF HIS SYSTEM.

"FOR THE MOST PART, HIS ATTACKS HAVE BEEN CENTERED ON HELLFIRE CLUB CHAPTER HOUSES...

"...AND I SAY GOOD RIDDANCE."

LONDON, ENGLAND.

THEIR BRAND OF KINK AND EVIL NEVER DID MUCH FOR ME.

IT WAS ALL A LITTLE TOO TAME.

"SOME WOULD SAY HE'S DOING THE WORLD A FAVOR, SCOURGING THE HELLFIRE CLUB THE WAY HE IS.

"AND ONCE HE FINDS WHO HE'S LOOKING FOR, HE'LL QUIET DOWN A BIT."

YOU KNOW WHERE SHE IS, DON'T YOU?

I HAVE MY SUSPICIONS.

I JUST THOUGHT I MIGHT VET THE ASSUMPTIONS BEFORE I POINTED ERIK IN THAT DIRECTION AND PULLED THE TRIGGER.

I LIKE YOU GUYS, OF COURSE, SO I'M WILLING TO SHARE WHAT I KNOW.

BUT I SHOULD WARN YOU...

"BECAUSE HE'S *HERE*."

32

KRA-SMASH!

I WISH YOU COULD UNDERSTAND, BOBBY.

I WISH YOU KNEW WHAT WAS GOING TO HAPPEN TO *YOU*.

I WISH YOU COULD KNOW WHAT I SAW...

...WHAT I DID...

YOU CAN'T *CHOKE* ME, ERIK...

...NOT WHILE I'M IN...

...MY *DIAMOND FORM*...

I DON'T PLAN ON *STRANGLING* YOU.

I DIDN'T COME HERE TO PLAY *GAMES*.

KRK!

SNAP!

SKRA-KA-KOW!

I'M SORRY ABOUT THIS. I REALLY AM.

HIS SHIELDS ARE DOWN.

TAKE HIM

HE'S TOO STRONG! IF WE'RE GOING TO STOP HIM, WE'LL NEED SOMETHING *MORE* THAN OUR MUTANT ABILITIES!

MY MAGIC--

I DON'T HAVE A CHOICE!

BEAST-- *DON'T!* YOU DON'T KNOW IF YOU CAN CONTROL IT!

BUT YOU *DO,* HENRY. UNLIKE ME, YOU HAVE NOTHING *BUT* CHOICES AHEAD OF YOU.

I'LL NOT SEE YOU MAKE THIS ONE--

--BECAUSE OF ME.

SLAM!

YOU *KILLED* HIM!

SHRAKKOW!

HE WILL *LIVE,* CYCLOPS.

I WOULD SPARE *EVERY* MUTANT, IF I COULD, SAVE THE WHITE QUEEN.

IT PAINS ME THAT YOU... IN WHOM I SAW THE *MOST* POTENTIAL...

...ARE BEYOND SAVING.

AH--

CRUNCH--

KRAK!

I KNEW TRUSTING YOU WAS A MISTAKE!

IT WAS YOU, ANGEL, WHO DIDN'T WANT TO STAY IN THIS WORLD.

AND NOW YOU FIGHT SO FIERCELY.

WHO DO YOU THINK WILL PROTECT MUTANTS WHEN YOU RETURN HOME?

SHRAAARKKL

ANGEL! I'VE GOT YOU!

GODDESS! I'VE GOT--

TELL ME WHAT I WANT TO KNOW.

IT'S THE ONLY WAY TO HELP THESE "INNOCENT" PEOPLE.

I KNOW WHAT'S IN YOUR HEAD, MAGNETO.

YOU LET ME IN...LET ME SEE.

I KNOW WHAT YOU ARE...AND I KNOW THERE'S LITTLE CHANCE OF STOPPING YOU...

...BUT I'LL BE *DAMNED* IF I'M BACKING DOWN.

I KNOW YOU WON'T, CHILD.

FOR ALL YOUR POWER, YOUR GREATEST STRENGTH...

...IS YOUR PERSEVERANCE...

....YOUR WILLINGNESS...

...TO *SACRIFICE* EVERYTHING AGAIN AND AGAIN...

...BUT I WILL NOT LET YOU OFFER YOURSELF UP TO ME.

IF WE CONTINUE THIS FIGHT...

...IF NEITHER OF US BACKS DOWN...

...THEN WE BOTH MIGHT DIE.

AND I CANNOT HAVE THAT.

WHEN THE WHITE QUEEN AND HER ALLIES ATTACKED ME...

...I KILLED MUTANTS TO SAVE MYSELF...

...I USED THE TIME PLATFORM...

...AND I SAW--

MAGNETO? YOU SAW... WHAT?

WHAT DID YOU SEE?

"WELL...THIS IS SIMPLY DREARY."

YOU REALIZE, OF COURSE, THAT MAGNETO WILL FIND ME.

I HAVE RESOURCES.

I HAVE MEANS.

THERE'S NO NEED TO MAKE ME STAY... HERE.

WE'RE NOT MAKING YOU DO ANYTHING. YOU'RE FREE TO GO WHENEVER YOU LIKE.

BUT I'D SUGGEST TAKING A LITTLE TIME TO HEAL.

WE CAN'T PROMISE YOU WE'LL BE AROUND TO HELP YOU NEXT TIME, THOUGH. OUR...TIME HERE IS GROWING SHORT, I'D IMAGINE.

I LIKE YOU BETTER WHEN YOU'RE OLDER.

JUST FOR A LITTLE WHILE, ALL RIGHT, EMMA?

AT SOME POINT...MAYBE...YOU AND MAGNETO MUST WORK THIS OUT WITHOUT KILLING EACH OTHER.

SCOTT'S RIGHT, YOU KNOW...

"...ONCE WE'RE GONE...

"...THE X-MEN ARE GOING TO NEED YOU BOTH."

THE FUTURE.

THIS IS THE WORLD I HAVE WROUGHT.

19 YEARS LATER.

I HAVE SHAPED IT AS SURELY AS I HAVE SHAPED METAL.

NEW YORK CITY.

AND, LIKE METAL, THIS WORLD HAS BEEN *TWISTED* TO SERVE MY PURPOSE.

I KNOW THIS INSTINCTIVELY.

EVEN THOUGH THIS IS THE FIRST TIME I HAVE VISITED THIS PLACE... THIS TIME...I KNOW.

I HAVE SEEN IT BEFORE.

"YOU *SAVED* THE MUTANTS.

"WHEN THE *REAVER VIRUS* FIRST APPEARED, THERE HAD BEEN NO SIGN OF YOU FOR YEARS.

"EVERYONE THOUGHT YOU WERE *DEAD*.

"THE *AVENGERS* TRIED TO STOP THE INFECTION FROM SPREADING.

"THE *X-MEN* TRIED, TOO.

IT STARTED AS *HATE*.

AND I KNOW WHAT HATE CAN *MUTATE* INTO.

AMEN.

SO HAS HE SPOKEN.

AMEN!

HE HAS *SAVED* US!

NO.

NOT LIKE THIS.

YOU WILL NOT HONOR MY ACTIONS AS SOMETHING *SACRED*--

WHEN I SENSED YOUR RETURN, I THOUGHT I HAD TO BE *MISTAKEN*.

I THOUGHT IT WAS SOME REMNANT OF A *BAD DREAM*.

I THOUGHT MY *FEARS* WERE SOMEHOW PLAYING *TRICKS* ON ME.

BUT NOW YOU'RE HERE AGAIN--

34

YOU'RE *WRONG!*

MAGNETO SAVED US!

HE DID WHAT NO ONE ELSE COULD DO.

HE DID WHAT NO ONE ELSE *WOULD* DO.

WE'RE ALIVE BECAUSE OF MAGNETO.

YOU...DON'T KNOW WHAT YOU'RE SAYING.

I'M SORRY.

YOU DON'T KNOW *ANYTHING* ABOUT HIM.

YOU DON'T KNOW WHO MAGNETO REALLY IS.

AND YOU DO, CYCLOPS?

IF YOU'VE NEVER RETURNED HOME, YOU'VE NOT SEEN ME AS AN *ENEMY.*

IN THE ERA YOU'VE EXISTED, I WAS AN *ALLY* TO YOU.

HOW OFTEN WERE YOUR IDEALS AND MINE IN OPPOSITION?

YOU CAN'T THROW TIME TRAVEL IN MY FACE, NOT WHEN YOU'RE OUTSIDE OF YOUR OWN TIME YOURSELF.

YOU ONLY KNOW WHAT YOU HAVE DONE IN YOUR *PAST.*

YOU DON'T KNOW WHAT YOU'RE *GOING TO DO* IN YOUR *FUTURE.*

THEN... MAYBE... THERE'S A WAY TO *FIX* THIS.

MAYBE THERE'S A WAY TO *SET THINGS RIGHT.*

NO, JEAN. THIS WILL NOT WORK OUT THE WAY YOU THINK.

THE WAY MAGNETO WOULD "FIX" THINGS--

THIS IS WHAT TURNS HIM INTO A *MONSTER.*

LEAVE HIM ALONE! HE SAVED US!

MAGNETO-- NOT THE X-MEN!

PERHAPS IT IS A MONSTER'S PROTECTION THAT MUTANTKIND NEEDS.

THIS ISN'T ABOUT PROTECTING MUTANTS.

THIS IS ABOUT YOUR OWN HUBRIS.

THIS IS YOU TRYING TO *PROVE* THAT EVERYTHING YOU'VE DONE IS *JUSTIFIED.*

FOR GOD'S SAKE--

"--WHO DO YOU THINK RAISED ALL THOSE DAMN STATUES?"

DAVIS   BYRNE

YOU DID IT. YOU DID IT TO PROVE SOMETHING. TO PROVE YOU WERE RIGHT!

WAS I?

MAYBE YOU WERE. MAYBE YOU WEREN'T.

IT HARDLY MATTERS NOW.

HANK... WE CAN'T--

WHEN YOU FACED ME BEFORE...

...WHEN YOU STOOD AGAINST ME IN THIS TIME...

...WHAT HAPPENED?

YOU *KILLED* ME, DIDN'T YOU?

TIME IS A STRANGE THING.

THE TIMELINE IS ALWAYS CORRECTING ITSELF. WE'VE SEEN THAT FIRSTHAND.

IF WE MAKE SURE YOU DO NOT RETURN TO YOUR TIMELINE, ALL OF THIS MIGHT CHANGE.

YOUR BEING HERE...MAYBE IT'S OUR CHANCE...TO FIX THINGS AFTER ALL.

YOU DON'T MEAN TO KEEP ME HERE.

WE... ...I... ...I SHOULDN'T HAVE LET YOU WALK OUT OF THAT SCRAPYARD...

WHEN YOU ASKED ME TO WORK WITH YOU...

...WHEN YOU LET ME READ YOUR MIND...

...I SHOULD HAVE *KILLED* YOU.

BUT YOU *DIDN'T.*

VRAAAAASH!

THIS, THEN, IS GOODBYE.

I APPRECIATE EVERYTHING YOU'VE DONE.

BUT WE MUST NOW PART WAYS.

FOR WHAT IT'S WORTH, MAGNETO...

...I RESPECT YOU FOR WHAT YOU'RE DOING...

...FOR EVERYTHING YOU'RE CASTING ASIDE.

I ADMIRE YOU.

AND I PITY YOU.

IT'S LIKELY THAT CHARLES PROGRAMMED YOU TO FEEL COMPASSION AND PITY.

THAT'S WHY YOU ARE NO LONGER OF USE TO ME.

WATCH AFTER THE X-MEN, DANGER.

I'M SURE YOU WOULD THINK SO.

THESE CREATIONS OF YOURS...

...THEY WOULD BE ABLE TO EXPERIENCE ALL THE EMOTIONS OF A LIVING BEING.

LOVE... SADNESS... FEAR... HOPE...

HATE.

I DON'T QUITE FOLLOW.

WHY WOULD WE EVER WANT A MACHINE TO EXPERIENCE HATE?

IN MY EXPERIENCE, *HATE* IS A PART OF *LIFE*.

I'VE SEEN FIRSTHAND WHAT YOUR EXPERIMENTS WILL YIELD.

IT'S LIKELY YOU'VE NEVER EVEN HEARD OF THE *REAVERS*...YOU COULDN'T CONCEIVE THE *HORRORS* YOU ARE GIVING BIRTH TO.

YOU MUST BE READY FOR *UNINTENDED CONSEQUENCES.*

THIS IS, AFTER ALL, YOUR *BRAINCHILD.*

IT WAS, YES, BUT NOW...

...WE'RE ALL PART OF IT...

...EVERYONE ON THE TEAM HAS BROUGHT SOMETHING NEW TO THE PROJECT.

OF COURSE.

AND SO, IT HAS COME TO THIS.

THIS IS THE FUTURE MOTHERVINE HAS WROUGHT.

NEW MUTANTS HAVE EMERGED.

AND THESE MUTANTS...NEED *GUIDANCE.*

I WILL NOT USE TIME TRAVEL TO ACCOMPLISH MY GOALS.

THE DANGERS ARE TOO GREAT.

I AM AN OLD MAN.

AND THE OLD WAYS, I FIND, WORK BEST.

TO ME, MY BROTHERHOOD.

35

--I REMEMBER.

I DON'T KNOW HOW.

MAYBE IT'S SOME SORT OF AFTER-EFFECT OF THE PHOENIX.

MAYBE I REMEMBER BECAUSE *YOU* REMEMBER.

MAYBE YOU'RE SUBCONSCIOUSLY *BROADCASTING* THE MEMORY, BEAMING IT STRAIGHT INTO MY HEAD.

MAYBE *YOU'RE* SCANNING MY THOUGHTS WITHOUT REALIZING IT.

SOUNDS LIKE US, HUH?

HAHA HAHAHA HAHA!

I WISH I HAD MORE TIME. I WISH *WE* HAD MORE TIME. I'D LIKE TO GET TO KNOW YOU A LITTLE BETTER...TO KNOW *ME* A LITTLE BETTER... BEFORE I GO BACK...

HOME.

YOU'VE MADE UP YOUR MIND, THEN?

I GUESS MY MIND'S BEEN MADE UP FOR ME.

THE FACT THAT WE'RE SITTING HERE TOGETHER...

...MEANS THAT WE GO BACK TO OUR TIMELINE SO THAT REALITY CAN TAKE THE SHAPE IT'S *SUPPOSED* TO TAKE.

IT MEANS...

...AS MUCH AS I LIKE BEING HERE WITH YOU...

...I WON'T REMEMBER ANY OF THIS...

...BECAUSE I NEED TO EXPERIENCE YOUR LIFE...

...OUR LIFE...

...FOR MYSELF.

SO, YEAH...

...I'VE DECIDED...

AND WHAT ABOUT THE OTHERS? WHAT DO THEY THINK ABOUT THAT?

ARE THEY *READY* TO GO HOME?

I DON'T KNOW IF *ANY* OF US ARE TRULY PREPARED.

HOW COULD WE BE?

IT'S NOT JUST ABOUT GOING BACK IN TIME.

IT'S ABOUT *BACKTRACKING.*

WE'VE ALL CHANGED SO MUCH.

WE BECAME OUR OWN PEOPLE.

AND ALL OF THAT... SOMEHOW... MUST BE *UNDONE*...

...SO THAT WE CAN BECOME *YOU.*

AND THAT'S A BAD THING?

I USED TO THINK SO.

I GUESS IT DEPENDS ON HOW YOU LOOK AT IT.

IF WE FORGET EVERYTHING THAT MAKES US WHO WE ARE...

...IF EVERYTHING THAT'S HAPPENED TO US JUST GETS... RESET...

...HOW'S THAT ANY *DIFFERENT* FROM *DYING?*

EVENTUALLY, YOU AND I WILL BE THE *SAME PERSON.*

BUT WE WON'T BE THE PERSON I AM *RIGHT NOW.*

THAT PERSON MUST *SACRIFICE* HERSELF...

I SEE.

I KNOW YOU, HANK. I KNOW *MYSELF*.

AND I FIND THAT HARD TO BELIEVE.

AND NOW YOU WANT ME TO SEND YOU BACK.

IT'S A LITTLE MORE COMPLICATED THAN THAT.

IF WE SIMPLY WANTED TO GO HOME, WE COULD DO THAT OURSELVES.

AFTER ALL, MAGNETO BUILT A *TIME MACHINE*.

WE NEED TO FIGURE OUT A WAY TO...

...UNDO...

...EVERYTHING THAT'S HAPPENED TO US.

MY MAGIC...

...JEAN'S POWERS... ANGEL'S...

...BOBBY...

AH, BOBBY.

HE DOESN'T LET ON.

BUT GOING BACK LIKE THIS...

"I COULDN'T CHANGE IF I TRIED."

THE FUTURE.

ALL RIGHT.

YOU'VE DONE IT, BOBBY DRAKE.

YOU'VE OFFICIALLY IMPRESSED ME.

OH, COME ON, CASON. DON'T ACT SO NONCHALANT

YOU WERE IMPRESSED BY ME WAY BEFORE NOW.

IS THAT WHAT PASSES FOR GAME AMONG THE X-MEN?

I KINDA GOT SOME POINTERS FROM GAMBIT.

MAYBE I SHOULD HAVE RETHOUGHT THAT.

DON'T WORRY.

IT'S CUTE.

DUMB BUT CUTE.

WHAT ABOUT THE FLOWERS AND THE GRASS AND THE TREES?

WHAT HAPPENS WHEN THE ICE MELTS?

YOU DIDN'T JUST KILL ALL THE PLANT LIFE WITH FROST TO WIN ME OVER, DID YOU?

OH. I GUESS I DID.

SO, YOU'RE ALL RIGHT WITH ALL THIS?

I MEAN, A LOT HAS--

ARE YOU ASKING IF I'M ALL RIGHT BEING *SOMEONE ELSE?*

THE ANSWER IS NO.

I'M FINE WITH GOING HOME. I MEAN, I DON'T WANT TO *BREAK REALITY* OR ANYTHING.

BUT I KNOW I WON'T BE MYSELF, NOT ANYMORE.

YOU KNOW, NO MATTER WHAT, YOU'LL *ALWAYS* BE YOURSELF.

EVEN IF YOU'RE THE ONLY ONE WHO KNOWS IT.

TIME TRAVEL'S NOT GOING TO TAKE THAT FROM YOU.

I GUESS.

IT JUST FEELS LIKE I'LL BE *LYING* TO EVERYONE AGAIN.

I'LL BE LYING TO *MYSELF.*

YOU'RE GOING TO GO ABOUT THIS IN YOUR OWN WAY AND IN YOUR OWN TIME.

I LOVE JEANNIE, BUT WHAT SHE DID...OUTING YOU...*US*...LIKE THAT...

...WELL, THAT WAS A LITTLE *MESSED UP.*

AND--LOOK-- YOU KNOW YOU'RE GONNA END UP *AWESOME.*

YEAH.

THING IS...

...I KIND OF FELT AWESOME BEING *ME.*

WHAT IS THIS?

WHO ARE ALL THESE...

...MUTANTS?

THESE ARE THE SLEEPERS.

THEY WERE IN XORN'S CARE.

AND NOW THEY ARE IN MINE.

WHICH MEANS THEY ARE IN YOURS.

MINE?

I CAN'T WATCH OUT FOR THEM.

I'M NOT STAYING.

AND EVEN IF I WERE, BEING SOME SORT OF MUTANT GUARDIAN...

SO, I GUESS WHAT I'M SAYING...

...IS GOODBYE.

WE HAVE A FEW MORE THINGS TO WRAP UP HERE ON EARTH...

...AND THEN...

...WELL, I GUESS WE'RE GONE.

YOU'RE *NOT* GONE, SON.

NOT BY A LONG SIGHT.

DAD--

I *KNOW* WHAT YOU'RE GOING TO SAY, SCOTT.

I KNOW, AND I STAND BY MY WORDS.

NOT BY A LONG SIGHT.

I WAS ALWAYS A *SCREWUP* AS A FATHER.

BUT YOU GAVE ME A CHANCE TO *FIX* THAT, SCOTT. YOU GAVE ME THE CHANCE TO SPEND TIME WITH YOU I *NEVER* THOUGHT I'D HAVE.

YOU TRAVEL IN SPACE LONG ENOUGH...

...YOU START TO GET A LITTLE *JADED*...

...BUT I DAMN WELL RECOGNIZE A *MIRACLE* WHEN ONE FINDS ITS WAY INTO MY LIFE.

THANKS, DAD. REALLY.

IT'S JUST THAT...IF WE DO THIS RIGHT...

...I WON'T EVEN *REMEMBER* ANY OF THIS.

AND THEN--

THIS TALK, YOU'LL CUT OUT!

REMEMBER, WE WILL!

ALWAYS!

HEPZIBAH'S RIGHT, CYCLOPS.

YOU'RE ONE OF US NOW AND FOREVER.

AND STARJAMMERS *NEVER* TRULY *DIE!*

WHAT DID I TELL YA, KIDDO?

NOT BY A LONG SIGHT.

WE'VE REBUILT THE MANSION HERE IN MADRIPOOR.

WE'VE GOT ALL THE AMENITIES.

AND I'VE GOT SOME APOLOGIES TO MAKE TO THE RAKSHA.

THE ONLY THING THAT IS MISSING IS STUDENTS.

...ABOUT THAT...

I THINK YOU GUYS REMEMBER DANGER AND POLARIS.

STUDENTS?

WE HAVE TRAINED ON THE STREETS OF MADRIPOOR.

THERE IS NOTHING YOU CAN TEACH US.

OOOOOH... DANGER LOVES A CHALLENGE.

WE'LL SEE.

IT'S NICE TO SEE THE TWO OF YOU TOGETHER LIKE THIS.

OH... ...WE'RE NOT... ...WE AREN'T...

BLOODSTORM?

I HOPE YOU DON'T MIND ME POKING MY NOSE WHERE IT DOESN'T BELONG. BUT I THINK I KNOW WHAT YOU'RE GOING THROUGH.

I'M NOT "GOING THROUGH" ANYTHING, HENRY.

OKAY...I'VE JUST LEARNED A PAINFUL LESSON IN MY TIME HERE.

AND THAT'S...

OH--
UNFINISHED BUSINESS.

BAMF

HEY.

IT'S WEIRD.

IT FEELS LIKE I SHOULD HAVE KNOWN YOU WERE THERE.

OUR PSYCHIC RAPPORT--

I KNOW.

IT'S BEEN SEVERED EVER SINCE THAT ORDEAL WITH THE POISONS, BUT--

--SOMETIMES IT FEELS LIKE IT'S STILL THERE.

WHAT DO YOU THINK THAT MEANS?

SCOTT--

--WHEN IT COMES TO ME AND YOU--

--THINKING TOO MUCH GETS US NOWHERE.

THAT'S THE TIME MACHINE THAT'LL SEND US HOME?

THIS ERA'S BEAST HAS BEEN MODIFYING IT BASED ON HIS ORIGINAL DESIGNS.

HE WANTS TO MAKE SURE THERE ARE NO *COMPLICATIONS* ONCE IT'S ACTIVATED.

THAT'S *CUTE.*

IT'S COMFORTING KNOWING THAT YOU *NEVER LEARN,* HANK.

THERE ARE *ALWAYS* COMPLICATIONS.

SPEAKING OF COMPLICATIONS.

WHAT ABOUT MY *WINGS?*

WHAT ABOUT ALL THE NEW MEMORIES AND SKILLS WE'VE PICKED UP?

WE CAN'T JUST GO BACK IN TIME...NOT LIKE WE ARE NOW.

YEAH.

WE'RE SURROUNDED BY *PSYCHICS, SCIENTISTS* AND *MYSTICS.*

WE'LL GET IT FIGURED OUT.

BREAKING NEWS OUT OF WASHINGTON, D.C.....